About Face

Taking Your Community by Force with Prayer

VOLUME 1

Lillian Joel

THIS BOOK IS PRESENTED TO

First Lady Sharon Patterson

BY

Lillian Joel

DATE

8-17-19

Thank you for praying for your community! Together We Con

ABOUT FACE

TAKING YOUR COMMUNITY BY FORCE WITH PRAYER

VOLUME 1

LILLIAN JOEL

Cover and book design by CreativeLog
Edited by Daynariffic

Contact Lillian Joel at (202) 681-5481

ISBN: 9781493682003

"If My people who are called by My name will humble themselves, and pray and seek My face, and turn from their wicked ways, then I will hear from heaven, and will forgive their sin and heal their land."

2 Chronicles 7:14

[23] For assuredly, I say to you, whoever says to this
mountain, 'Be removed and be cast into the sea,'
and does not doubt in his heart, but believes that
those things he says will be done, he will have
whatever he says. [24] Therefore I say to you,
whatever things you ask when you pray, believe that
you receive them, and you will have them.

Mark 11:23-24

The heaven of heavens is for God, but He puts us in charge of the earth.

Psalm 115:16 MSG

And from the days of John the Baptist until now the kingdom of heaven suffers violence and the violent take it by force.

Matthew 11:12

ACKNOWLEDGMENTS

First and foremost I want to thank God for helping me complete this book! I must admit it was quite a challenge with the ongoing time thieves I allowed to delay the process, but nevertheless, it is finished!

I would like to thank my daughter, Brittney Capers and my mom Barbara Watkins for having faith in me to get this God ordained assignment completed. I love and appreciate you guys so much for all your love and support!

Thank you Rose Matthews for your assistance with the community prayer calls that inspired me to write this book.

Thank you to Melanie Bonita for being so dedicated and determined to keep me on track in getting this masterpiece to print! You are truly a godsend and I appreciate you and your tenacity!

Special thanks to my Pastors Michael and Deloris Freeman of Spirit of Faith Christian Center for teaching me the Word of God with simplicity and with a spirit of faith. You guys are the best!

Finally, I'd like to thank all these people that probably don't know how they have inspired me while doing their own thing: Clo Taylor, Conya Bailey, Stacy Evans, Stacey Milam, Cynthia Washington, Robyn Smith, Cheryl Wood, Theresa Royal Brown, Candice Camille, my awesome photographer, Jackie Hicks and Vicki Irwin. You guys rock in your own right and I thank you for being the great people you are! Keep on doing what you're doing!

Table of Contents

Introduction

Did you know that prayer has power? The Bible tells us that the effectual, fervent prayer of the righteous avails much. That's who we are, the righteousness of God! We are not righteous because of what we have done, but what Jesus has done on our behalf.

Jesus is the great intercessor and if you are reading this book, I believe you too have a heart and desire to intercede on behalf of others, particularly, your community!

As an intercessor we must be willing to surrender ourselves to God ~ all of ourselves: heart, mind, soul and spirit. We have to be persistent, consistent, patient, self-disciplined and strategic. We have to have the heart, mind and eyes of God to see people as He does.

When we pray, we must put God in remembrance of His word knowing that it will not return to Him void and that it will accomplish the thing for which it has been sent. Our motives must always be right so that we never pray amiss - therefore knowing that our prayers will be answered!

It's imperative that we spend quality time with our Father on a daily basis, and meditate on His word day and night. We must make God and His Word (which are one) final authority in our lives.

The Bible says let everything that has breath praise the Lord and as intercessors we must always praise and worship God. Our worship silences the enemy and our God inhabits the praises of His people! As prayer warriors we magnify and glorify God at all times and His praises shall continually be in our mouths.

We must stand fast in faith as we pray. It's the trick of the enemy to make situations appear worse when we pray, but we must walk by faith and not by sight. We cannot be moved by what we see with our natural eyes, but choose to see with our spiritual eyes, knowing that everything is already alright! Remember, without faith it is impossible to please God!

As we collectively intercede on behalf of our communities know that every prayer is packed with the Word of God and there is enough power packed in the Word to perform. We are standing in agreement according to Matthew 18:19-20 where Jesus said, "If two of us agree on earth concerning anything that we ask, it will be done for us by our Father in heaven. For where two or three are gathered together in His name, He is in the midst of them. Although we may not be in the same room, we are in the same spirit and NOTHING can penetrate it.

We are also standing on 1 John 5:14-15 knowing that this is the confidence that we have in Him, that if we ask anything according to His will, He hears us. And since we know that He hears us, whatever we ask, we know that we have the petitions that we have asked of Him.

Lastly, we are standing on Isaiah 55:11 where God said "So shall My word be that goes forth from My mouth, it shall not return to Me void, but it shall accomplish that which I please and it shall prosper in the thing for which I sent it."

So let's do an ***About Face*** and turn our communities around with the Kingdom of Light; eradicating and disseminating all powers of darkness because we believe we receive when we pray in Jesus Name! Glory to God!

MEDITATION SCRIPTURES

"And I also say to you that you are Peter, and on this rock I will build my church, and the gates of Hades shall not prevail against it. And I will give you the keys of the kingdom of heaven; whatever you bind on earth will be bound in heaven, and whatever you loose on earth will be loosed in heaven."

Matthew 16:18-19

"And whenever you stand praying, if you have anything against anyone, forgive him, that your Father in heaven may also forgive you your trespasses."

Mark 11:25

"Finally, my brethren, be strong in the Lord and in his mighty power. Put on the whole armor of God, that you may be able to stand against the wiles of the devil. For we do not wrestle against flesh and blood, but against principalities, against powers, against the rulers of the darkness of this age, against spiritual hosts of wickedness in the heavenly places.

Ephesians 6:10-12

"Most assuredly, I say to you, he who believes in Me, the works that I do he will do also; and greater works than these he will do, because I go to My Father. And whatever you ask in My name, that I will do that the Father may be glorified in the Son. If you ask anything in My name, I will do it."

John 14:12-14

"If you abide in Me, and My words abide in you, you will ask what you desire, and it shall be done for you.

John 15:7

"For with God nothing will be impossible."

Luke 1:37

OUR PRAYER FOR INTERCESSORS

Thank You Father for the Intercessors throughout the world that are using this book to pray to You on behalf of our communities. They have a heart for Your people and desire transformation within all communities by the Word of God. Their hunger and thirst for righteousness in our land will permeate heaven and be a sweet aroma to Your nostrils. They move Your hands with their compassion for advancement and resurrection of all communities.

We decree the intercessors are increased a thousand times more in every area of their lives and that they live victorious lives in and through You. Every need they have is already met and they always stay in a state of expectancy. They walk in favor with You and man all the days of their lives.

We decree that they are redeemed from sickness and disease which is a curse of the law, and are equipped to overcome all the fiery darts and trickery of the enemy.

Thank You Father that Angels are encamped about them and their families keeping watch over them from all hurt, harm, and danger. No weapon formed against them shall ever prosper and every tongue that rises up against them in judgment they shall condemn. We thank You that their foot is not made to stumble and everything they set themselves to do will prosper.

Thank You for Your goodness and mercy that is following them all the days of their lives.

We declare that every intercessor will live limitless lifestyles and whatever they believe possible for them is possible as they stand on Your word. We decree that their personal prayer lives are increased the more and You get the glory in all they do. The Greater One lives on the inside of them and they cannot fail.

Father we thank You for the faith of all intercessors throughout the earth. We believe we receive when we pray in Jesus Name, Amen.

SCRIPTURE REFERENCES

May the LORD God of your fathers make you a thousand times more numerous than you are, and bless you as He has promised you!

Deuteronomy 1:11 NKJV

And my God shall supply all your need according to His riches in glory by Christ Jesus.

Philippians 4:19

And Jesus increased in wisdom and stature, and in favor with God and men.

Luke 2:52

The angel of the LORD encamps all around those who fear Him, and delivers them.

Psalm 34:7

No weapon formed against you shall prosper, and every tongue w*hich* rises against you in judgment, You shall condemn. This *is* the heritage of the servants of the LORD, and their righteousness *is* from Me," says the LORD.

Isaiah 54:17

Then you will walk safely in your way, and your foot will not stumble.

Proverbs 3:23

Therefore keep the words of this covenant, and do them, that you may prosper in all that you do.

Deuteronomy 29:9

Surely goodness and mercy shall follow me all the days of my life; and I will dwell in the house of the Lord Forever.

Psalm 23:6

You are of God, little children, and have overcome them, because He who is in you is greater than he who is in the world.

1 John 4:4

The Power of Prayer in Our Communities

Father we thank You for the power of prayer. We know that the effectual, fervent prayer of the righteous avails much. And as the righteous we decree that our prayers are changing the face of all communities for Your glory this day!

When we pray Father we are putting You in remembrance of Your word, and we know that every word that You have spoken shall not return unto You void. That's why we choose not to be anxious for anything, but in everything by prayer and supplication we make our request known unto You.

So Father we request that Your presence in our communities is received by the people of our communities. We request that the blood of Jesus cover Your people and their minds be renewed with the Word of God. We request that You are placing people in our communities that have a heart for Your people that are not afraid to share the goodness of Jesus Christ. We request that every yoke of bondage be removed in the lives of the people in our communities and be replaced with Your yoke which is easy and Your burdens which are light because they choose to link up with You.

That our communities' cares and concerns are now Yours. We request that every need is met in our communities and as we pray, change has come to our communities.

We thank you for peace that surpasses all understanding and divine protection within our communities. We thank you that no weapon formed in our communities or against our communities shall ever prosper. We decree that grace and mercy are following the residents, business owners, workers, and the like all the days of their lives.

We decree that the power of prayer in our communities has manifested now, because we believe we receive when we pray in Jesus Name, Amen.

Scripture References

Confess your trespasses to one another, and pray for one another, that you may be healed. The effective, fervent prayer of a righteous man avails much.

James 5:16

So shall My word be that goes forth from My mouth; it shall not return to Me void, but it shall accomplish what I please, and it shall prosper in the thing for which I sent it.

Isaiah 55:11

"Ask, and it will be given to you; seek, and you will find; knock, and it will be opened to you.

Matthew 7:7

And whatever things you ask in prayer, believing, you will receive.

Matthew 21:22

And whatever you ask in My name, that I will do, that the Father may be glorified in the Son. If you ask anything in My name, I will do it.

John 14:13-14

Be anxious for nothing, but in everything by prayer and supplication, with thanksgiving, let your requests be made known to God; and the peace of God, which surpasses all understanding, will guard your hearts and minds through Christ Jesus.

Philippians 4:6-7

No weapon formed against you shall prosper, and every tongue which rises against you in judgment You shall condemn. This is the heritage of the servants of the LORD, and their righteousness is from Me," Says the LORD.

Isaiah 54:17

The Power of Renewing Our Minds for Our Communities

Father we thank You for the renewal of the minds of everyone in our communities. Your Word tells us not to be conformed to this world; but be ye transformed by the renewing of our mind, that we may prove what is that good, and acceptable, and perfect, will of Yours. We pray that the minds of the people in our communities are being renewed on a daily basis. Our prayer for them is to renew their minds by reading, meditating, and speaking Your Word on a consistent basis. We pray that their minds are not polluted and clear from anything that would hurt or weaken them spiritually. We decree that they think on things that are pure, lovely, just, of a good report, virtuous and praiseworthy.

Father we pray that they cast down imaginations, and every high thing that exalts itself against the knowledge of You and bring into captivity every thought to the obedience of Christ. We thank You that they choose to think about the good things, and refuse thoughts that are inappropriate. When wrong thoughts and desires come, we decree that people will be swift to respond by speaking Your Word over themselves and over their situations.

We pray that they will not let doubt, worry, or fear contaminate their minds. For You have not given us a spirit of fear, but of power, love and a sound mind. We decree that they cast all their care on You for You care for them.

We thank You in advance for perfecting the things which concern our communities.

Father we pray that the people of our communities refuse to fill their minds with the poison of gossip, backbiting, and jealousy. They will keep their hearts with all diligence, for out of it spring the issues of life and they will put away a deceitful mouth and put perverse lips far from them. We pray they will guard and protect their minds by not watching, reading, or listening to anything that is not pleasing to You. Although we live in a society where it appears that everything goes, we decree that people are now looking to You for new direction. That their old ways of thinking about going to church and hearing the word is hindered and we decree an unsettled spirit in them until they serve You. We thank You that churches will be filled with Your people flooding the altars wanting a change in their lives like never before and we set ourselves to be the light in this earth that will draw them unto You Father.

We pray that their eyes are enlightened to the truth of Your Word and that they walk in Your wisdom for every area of their lives. We decree that they make quality decisions and meditate on Your Word keeping their minds pure and undefiled, that they may be receptive to Your voice and ever ready to do Your will.

Father we thank You that they let the Word of Christ dwell in them richly and they allow the Word to permeate their hearts. We pray that they become members of Bible based churches so they can hear, learn and do the Word taught, so that they can walk out this prayer.

Father we thank you that they throw off their old sinful nature and their former way of life, which is corrupted by lust and deception and instead, let the Spirit renew their thoughts and attitudes, that they put on their new nature, created to be like You—truly righteous. They must put off their own self-centered thinking by confessing, repenting and casting its care over to You.

Father as Your people go through this renewal process we decree that they let patience have her perfect work, that they may be perfect and entire, wanting nothing. Although we know manifestations can happen suddenly we want to cover those that may not experience a suddenly and decree that the people of our communities will not get weary while doing well for they will reap if they faint not.

Father we bind every satanic attack, plot, plan and scheme of the enemy to get people off course. We loose Your loving grace and Christ's resurrection power upon these communities, giving them the ability to be all that You have called them to be and do all that You have called them to do and to have all that You have called them to have!

Father we thank you for the manifestation of renewed minds in our communities. We believe we receive when we pray in Jesus Name, Amen.

SCRIPTURE REFERENCES

And do not be conformed to this world, but be transformed by the renewing of your mind, that you may prove what *is* that good and acceptable and perfect will of God.

Romans 12:2

Finally, brethren, whatever things are true, whatever things *are* noble, whatever things *are* just, whatever things *are* pure, whatever things *are* lovely, whatever things *are* of good report, if *there is* any virtue and if *there is* anything praiseworthy—meditate on these things.

Philippians 4:8

…casting down arguments and every high thing that exalts itself against the knowledge of God, bringing every thought into captivity to the obedience of Christ

2 Corinthians 10:5

Keep your heart with all diligence, for out of it *spring* the issues of life.

Proverbs 4:23

Let the word of Christ dwell in you richly in all wisdom, teaching and admonishing one another in psalms and hymns and spiritual songs, singing with grace in your hearts to the Lord.

Colossians 3:16

[22]You were taught, with regard to your former way
of life, to put off your old self, which is being
corrupted by its deceitful desires; [23] to be made new
in the attitude of your minds; [24] and to put on the
new self, created to be like God in true
righteousness and holiness.

Ephesians 4:22-24 (NIV)

But let patience have *its* perfect work, that you may be perfect and complete, lacking nothing.

James 1:4

The Power of God in Our Communities

Father we thank You for who You are in our communities. Although there may be trouble around us, we are not moved by it. When we think of who You are and all that You have done on our behalf, we just say thank You!

Father You are our very present help in a time of trouble. Within our communities You are our strength. You are our peace. You are our refiner. You are the lifter of our heads when we allow life to get to us. We find comfort in You and Your word. You purify us and purge us and as we abide in You, You abide in us.

Thank you for giving us Your Son who is our power and wisdom. Jesus' name alone has the power to save, to deliver, to heal, to provide, to protect, to set free!

You Father are our resting place whenever we feel lost. You are our refuge and our strong tower. When we run to You , we are safe!

You are the one and only God we know that can and will change the face of our communities. You are love and Your love is never ending. We love You Father with all our heart, with all our soul, with all our mind and with all our strength. You are a mighty God and we are ever so grateful to love and serve You by loving and serving our communities.

We speak Your name with reverence and thanksgiving. We know that You answer the call and needs of Your people and we call You to our communities this day.

We call on You for guidance, direction, and covering. We plead the blood of Jesus over our communities. We want Your light to shine through us ever so brightly that our good works will glorify You and cause men to repent.

We know that You are our everlasting light and that all days of sorrow will come to an end. You are our hope of a bright future for the rest of our lives and our trust is in You.

Father we thank You for being everything we need in our communities. We believe we receive when we pray in Jesus Name, Amen.

SCRIPTURE REFERENCES

God *is* our refuge and strength, a very present help in trouble.

Psalm 46:1

"I am the vine, you *are* the branches. He who abides in Me, and I in him, bears much fruit; for without Me you can do nothing."

John 15:5

Then Peter said, "Silver and gold I do not have, but what I do have I give you: In the name of Jesus Christ of Nazareth, rise up and walk."

Acts 3:6

And this she did for many days. But Paul, greatly annoyed, turned and said to the spirit, "I command you in the name of Jesus Christ to come out of her." And he came out that very hour.

Acts 16:18

But to those called by God to salvation, both Jews and Gentiles, Christ is the power of God and the wisdom of God.

1 Corinthians 1:24

Let your light so shine before men, that they may see your good works and glorify your Father in heaven.

Matthew 5:16

The name of the LORD *is* a strong tower; the righteous run to it and are safe.

Proverbs 18:10

The Power of Praying in the Spirit for Our Communities*

Father according to the New Testament, Jesus wants to baptize everybody on earth with the Holy Spirit. He wants everybody on earth to speak in tongues and that's what we want to do for our communities. We decree we have the power from on High to do the works of God in our communities as we speak in tongues. We want to be edified as we speak in an unknown tongue. The word says that he that speaks in an unknown tongue edifies himself. As we speak in tongues, we are building ourselves up to the point that we can believe God instead of our circumstances and what's going on in and around our communities.

As we line our innermost being up with the power of speaking in tongues, the words we speak out of our mouths will line up with Your words.

We choose to communicate with You Father in our heavenly language according to Your word.

We thank You Father for this power of speaking in tongues. We know that as we are speaking to You and building ourselves up, we are changing the atmosphere of our communities; we are breaking down strongholds and binding all satanic attacks of destruction and despair within our communities. We are in Your perfect will as we speak in tongues and are bearing fruit.

We believe Your word Father and take full authority over the devil. We know that as we speak in tongues we have Your spirit and power in us to do all that You have called us to do on behalf of our communities.

Thank You Father for Holy Spirit who is our comforter and guide as He abides in us forever.

We choose this day to make speaking in tongues our lifestyle. We decree supernatural results are taking place in our communities right now.

Father we thank You for the ability to speak in tongues and the power it has to change our communities. We believe we receive when we pray in Jesus Name, Amen.

*PRAYER FOR BAPTISM OF HOLY SPIRIT WITH EVIDENCE OF SPEAKING IN TONGUES

Father Your word says in Luke 11:13 "If you then, being evil, know how to give good gifts to your children, how much more will your heavenly Father give the Holy Spirit to those who ask Him!" So I ask you in the name of Jesus to fill me with the Holy Spirit. Holy Spirit rise up within me as I praise God. I fully expect to speak with other tongues as You give me the utterance according to Acts 2:4. I believe I receive in Jesus Name, Amen!

Begin to praise God for filling you with Holy Spirit. Speak those words and syllables you receive – not in your own language, but the language given to you by Holy Spirit. You have to use your own voice. God will not force you to speak. Don't be concerned with how it sounds. It's a heavenly language!

SCRIPTURE REFERENCES

But you shall receive power when the Holy Spirit has come upon you; and you shall be witnesses to Me in Jerusalem, and in all Judea and Samaria, and to the end of the earth."

Acts 1:8

He who speaks in a tongue edifies himself...

1 Corinthians 14:4

Pray at all times (on every occasion, in every season) in the Spirit, with all [manner of] prayer and entreaty. To that end keep alert and watch with strong purpose *and* perseverance, interceding in behalf of all the saints (God's consecrated people).

Ephesians 6:18 (AMP)

So too the [Holy] Spirit comes to our aid *and* bears us up in our weakness; for we do not know what prayer to offer *nor* how to offer it worthily as we ought, but the Spirit Himself goes to meet our supplication *and* pleads in our behalf with unspeakable yearnings and groanings too deep for utterance.

Romans 8:26 (AMP)

The Power of Fasting for Our Communities

Father in the name of Jesus we choose to fast on behalf of our communities. We know that fasting is a part of our lifestyle as believers.

Our fasting will bring our flesh under subjection, therefore making us pliable to the purpose and plan You have for our communities. As we draw closer to You Father, You will draw closer to us!

As we set ourselves apart during our time of fasting, we decree that our hearts are ready to obey and our ears are set to hear Holy Spirit as He leads, guides and directs our steps within our communities. We decree that our fasting will penetrate the barriers that are blocking the flow of the blessing throughout our communities.

We declare that doors shall be opened for greater opportunities, eyes will be enlightened to the knowledge of You and that there will be a sudden revealing, removing and exposing of anything that is not of You within our communities. We shall be called the repairer of the breach and the restorer of the streets. Our communities will never be the same.

We decree that the gates of hell shall not prevail against our communities because we chose to fast and pray.

We believe we receive when we pray that the power of fasting has changed our communities in Jesus Name, Amen.

SCRIPTURE REFERENCES

But I discipline my body and bring it into subjection, lest, when I have preached to others, I myself should become disqualified.

1 Corinthians 9:27

Is this not the fast that I have chosen; to loose the bonds of wickedness, to undo the heavy burdens, to let the oppressed go free, and that you break every yoke?

Isaiah 58:6

Those from among you shall build the old waste places; you shall rise up the foundations of many generations; and you shall be called the Repairer of the Breach, The Restorer of Streets to Dwell in.

Isaiah 58:12

"Moreover, when you fast, do not be like the hypocrites, with a sad countenance. For they disfigure their faces that they may appear to men to be fasting. Assuredly, I say to you, they have their reward. "But you, when you fast, anoint your head and wash your face, so that you do not appear to men to be fasting, but to your Father who is in the secret place; and your Father who sees in secret will reward you openly."

Matthew 6:16-18

The Power of Forgiving Past Transgressions within Our Communities

Father we decree that everyone will walk in total forgiveness of the transgressions that have taken place in our communities.

There may be folks that have done some things that are not pleasing to You, and perhaps have hurt their fellow neighbors with their actions, but we now cover this in prayer.

We bind the things on earth that we do not want and loose the things that we do want. So we bind the remembrance of past transgressions and loose forgiveness in our communities.

We choose to trust You and thank You in everything. Although the appearance of a thing may not be favorable with the natural eye, we know that all things, our praying, fasting and speaking in tongues are working together for the good of our communities.

Father we choose not to hold people hostage regarding their past transgressions. We pray that they have a repentant heart and just as You've cast their sin as far as the east is from the west and remember them no more, so do we. We are not the judge and jury of Your people, but we do judge believers according to Your word. We stand on

Your word and not of our own understanding.

We take this opportunity again to loose forgiveness of past transgressions within our communities to all. We bind the remembrance of those hurtful things and render them powerless as we move forward in the things of God. We refuse to allow Satan to have a foot hold in our minds regarding the past so we cast it down now for our communities, in the name of Jesus.

We take authority over our communities and thank You Father for newness of life and strength of Your people so they are not easily swayed by the temptation to keep past transgressions not only of themselves, but of others, prevalent in their lives. They will walk in boldness and confidence as they give themselves to You and walk in Your ways.

We are committed to change the face of our communities and it starts with forgiveness of past transgressions as we walk in total restoration.

Have Your way Father like never before in the lives of Your people. We choose to have a heart like Yours in the earth that will make a mark in the lives of Your people that can never be erased.

Father we thank You for the ability to forgive our past transgressions within our communities. We believe we receive when we pray in Jesus Name, Amen.

Scripture References

[14] "For if you forgive men their trespasses, your heavenly Father will also forgive you. [15] But if you do not forgive men their trespasses, neither will your Father forgive your trespasses.

Matthew 6:14-15

As far as the east is from the west, *so* far has He removed our transgressions from us.

Psalm 103:12

"If you forgive someone's sins, they're gone for good. If you don't forgive sins what are you going to do with them?"

John 20:23 MSG

"So My heavenly Father also will do to you if each of you, from his heart, does not forgive his brother his trespasses."

Matthew 18:35

"And I will give you the keys of the kingdom of heaven, and whatever you bind on earth will be bound in heaven, and whatever you loose on earth will be loosed in heaven."

Matthew 16:19

The Power of Love in Our Communities

Father in the name of Jesus we decree that the power of love is evident in our communities. Your Word says that love never fails. We know that without love, our giving will not work, tongues and prophecy will not work, faith fails and knowledge is unfruitful.

Have Your way Father in the lives of the people of our communities. We decree that the agape love of God is spread abroad in our communities like never before. Father we know that Your promises are yes and Amen and as we pray Your word back to You, we know that it will not return void. We bind the spirit of hatred in our communities. We thank You that love is eradicating every demonic force that has reared its ugly head in our communities.

We work the power of love in our communities. Kindness is on the lips of our communities. Gratitude is evidenced in our communities. Humility is perfected in our communities. Gentleness and self-control is popular within our communities. We choose to exercise the fruit of the Spirit and be the light in our communities that will never weaken or faint.

We decree that the love of God that is shed abroad in our hearts is our motivation and inspiration in our communities. We overcome every situation in our communities with God's love which cannot fail.

We overturn all hatred, jealousy, envy, strife, dissention, division, gossip and the like, with the power of love!

There is no fear in love, but perfect love casts out fear.

We thank You Father for the manifestation of agape love with everyone in our communities. We believe we receive when we pray, in Jesus name, Amen!

SCRIPTURE REFERENCES

1 Though I speak with the tongues of men and of
angels, but have not love, I have become sounding
brass or a clanging cymbal. 2 And though I have *the
gift of* prophecy, and understand all mysteries and
all knowledge, and though I have all faith, so that I
could remove mountains, but have not love, I am
nothing. 3 And though I bestow all my goods to feed
the poor, and though I give my body to be burned,
but have not love, it profits me nothing. 4 Love
suffers long *and* is kind; love does not envy; love
does not parade itself, is not puffed up; 5 does not
behave rudely, does not seek its own, is not
provoked, thinks no evil; 6 does not rejoice in
iniquity, but rejoices in the truth; 7 bears all things,
believes all things, hopes all things, endures all
things.

8 Love never fails. But whether *there are*
prophecies, they will fail; whether *there are*
tongues, they will cease; whether *there is*
knowledge, it will vanish away. 9 For we know in
part and we prophesy in part. 10 But when that
which is perfect has come, then that which is in part
will be done away. 11 When I was a child, I spoke as
a child, I understood as a child, I thought as a child;
but when I became a man, I put away childish
things. 12 For now we see in a mirror, dimly, but

then face to face. Now I know in part, but then I shall know just as I also am known. [13] And now abide faith, hope, love, these three; but the greatest of these *is* love.

1 Corinthians 13:1-13

The Power of Fellowship within Our Communities

Father as we walk in the agape love that You have for us, we partner with You and bestow agape love to our neighbors and other patrons throughout our community.

It is imperative that we not stay in our comfort zones, but show ourselves friendly as we branch out to meet the needs of others. As we are led by You Father, we will open ourselves to fellowshipping within our communities. Whether it's a word in due season, or a much needed smile of encouragement, we choose to make an impact.

As we stand in the confidence of knowing that You are backing us to the hilt in our endeavors, there isn't anything we worry about when fellowshipping within our communities. We cast all our care on You because we know that You care for us! We know that angels are encamped about us and they are keeping watch over us from any hurt, harm or danger.

Father although our fellowship may seem abnormal to some, we choose to be abnormal in this day and time. We know that Your ways and thoughts are not the same of those that do not share our faith in our communities, but we choose to break the barriers and bring love and kindness to the forefront of our communities. We choose to stand on Your word and bring people up to Your level, instead of watering down Your word and ways to fit them.

We are doers of Your word and it's the doers of Your word that are blessed. So as we fellowship we decree lives are changed, homes are changed, finances are changed and communities are changed for Your glory!

The days of just doing business as usual are over in our communities. We fellowship with a smile and lend our ears and hearts to Your people graciously.

Have Your way Father in our time of fellowship within our communities. We believe we receive when we pray, in Jesus Name, Amen!

SCRIPTURE REFERENCES

A man who has friends must himself be friendly, but there is a friend who sticks closer than a brother.

Proverbs 18:24

A man has joy by the answer of his mouth, and a word *spoken* in due season, how good it is!

Proverbs 15:23

...casting all your care upon Him, for He cares for you.

1 Peter5:7

As iron sharpens iron, so a man sharpens the countenance of his friend.

Proverbs 27:17

For God has not given us a spirit of fear, but of power and of love and of a sound mind.

2 Timothy 1:7

The Power of Eradicating Deception in our Communities

Father in the name of Jesus we come against all power of deception. We have total authority and dominion over anything that doesn't line up with the Word of God. There is coming a day, when even the elect will be deceived and we must hold fast to our confession and profession of faith knowing that we are over comers in every area of our lives.

We choose to avoid worldly wisdom by thinking we are wise in our own right, but ask for Your wisdom. We choose to lean and rely on You because You are our source. As we draw near to You during our times of prayer and fellowship, You draw nearer to us.

We exchange our weakness for Your strength during times of deception. What the enemy meant for evil You will turn it for our good. We decree all the conditions of our communities are favorable and there isn't anything Satan can do about it.

We refuse to be deceived any longer. We know that You are not mocked Father, and whatsoever we sow, that we will reap. So we choose to sow the fruit of the spirit which is love, joy, peace, longsuffering, kindness, goodness, faithfulness, gentleness and self-control.

We thank You Father for revealing and exposing all hidden things, every source of wrong prayer, trickery and deceit and that they are driven out and thrown into the abyss with all its lies, effects, adverse effects, and stings never to return in the name of Jesus. Let the veil of deception be removed so that we can see through the haze, smoke screens and plots of the wicked one and let the truth of Your Word be made manifest in our communities.

We decree that we are strong in the Lord and in the power of His might; putting on the whole armor of God that we are able to stand against the wiles of the devil. We know that we are not wrestling against flesh and blood, but against principalities, against powers, against the rulers of the darkness of this age, against spiritual hosts of wickedness in the heavenly places. So we take up the whole armor of God so that we are able to withstand in the evil day, and having done all, to stand.

We know that our feet are not made to stumble and in everything we give thanks. We thank You for Holy Spirit who leads, guides and directs us into all truth. We thank You that He tells us things to come and we are positioned to receive His teachings. We are not moved by what we see and what we hear;
we are only moved by the Word of God. We choose to use the Word as our final authority and walk in boldness and confidence knowing that we have the victory in every area of our lives.

We decree that deception is eradicated in our communities. We believe we receive when we pray, in Jesus Name, Amen!

SCRIPTURE REFERENCES

And Jesus answered and said to them: "Take heed that no one deceives you.

Matthew 24:4

For whatever is born of God overcomes the world. And this is the victory that has overcome the world—our faith.

1 John 5:4

Draw near to God and He will draw near to you.

James 4:8a

Do not be deceived, God is not mocked; for whatever a man sows, that he will also reap.

Galatians 6:7

Put on the whole armor of God, that you may be able to stand against the wiles of the devil.

Ephesians 6:11

When you walk, your steps will not be hindered, and when you run, you will not stumble.

Proverbs 4:12

The Power of Faith & Patience in Our Communities

Father we thank You for Your word for our provision. We decree that we exercise both faith and patience in our communities and are not so quick to give up, waver and faint. We choose not to become weary for we know that the promise is ours. We decree that in the day of adversity, our strength will not fail us.

Father we thank You that we walk by faith and not by sight in our communities. We walk in the boldness and confidence, knowing that what we believe and pray will come to pass. As we pray for our communities we let patience have her perfect work. We are not moved by what we see, what we hear, or what's being said, we are only moved by the word of God.

Father we decree that everything we have prayed and will continue to pray is being made manifest right now in the name of Jesus. Your word says that if we have faith the size of a mustard seed, we can move mountains. We move the mountains that are hindering forward progress in our communities. We move the mountain of unbelief. We move the mountain of complacency. We move the mountain of impatience and irritability. We move the mountain of fear. And we move the mountain of doubt. Our faith and patience will allow us to see Your promises of Yes and Amen. We render all opposing forces powerless and unfruitful.

We decree that the wonder twins of faith and patience have their way in our communities like never before. We believe we receive when we pray, in Jesus Name, Amen!

Scripture References

[2] My brethren, count it all joy when you fall into various trials, [3] knowing that the testing of your faith produces patience. [4] But let patience have *its* perfect work, that you may be perfect and complete, lacking nothing.

James 1:2-4

[11] And we desire that each one of you show the same diligence to the full assurance of hope until the end, [12] that you do not become sluggish, but imitate those who through faith and patience inherit the promises.

Hebrews 6:11-12

And let us not grow weary while doing good, for in due season we shall reap if we do not lose heart.

Galatians 6:9

For assuredly, I say to you, whoever says to this mountain, 'Be removed and be cast into the sea,' and does not doubt in his heart, but believes that those things he says will be done, he will have whatever he says.

Mark 11:23

The Power of Overcoming Fear within Our Communities

Father thank You for not giving us a spirit of fear, but of power, love and a sound mind. We bind the spirit of fear that wants to take hold in our communities. We decree that Your word has final authority in our lives and we walk in total and complete trust and confidence in You.

Father You've shown us time and time again in Your word that You will never leave us or forsake us. As You were with Moses, Abraham, Hagar, Joshua and a host of others, so are You within our communities imploring us not to fear.

We choose not to let worry consume us in any area of our lives. We are casting our care, concern, worry and fear on You. Your word says to not let our hearts be troubled or afraid, and to keep our mind focused on You, and You will keep us in perfect peace.

When things happen in our communities Father, we choose not to be moved, and we move the situations with our prayer and praise of Your goodness and mercy. Though a thousand may fall at one side and ten thousand at the other, it will not harm us. We take full authority of the dominance You have given us in the earth.

Your word says, whatever we bind on earth would be bound in heaven and whatever we loose on earth shall be loosed in heaven. So Father we bind the fear of lack, insufficiency, sickness, and death. We render them powerless and of no effect in our communities. We bind you Satan for infiltrating our communities with these fears and we loose renewed minds on God's people concerning fear.

We are strong and of good courage and do not fear because You are with us in our communities. We choose to renew our minds daily to Your word so that the stagnate, gripping power of fear is eradicated in our communities. We choose to walk in peace and love and to walk by faith and not by sight.

So it is this day and forever more we have overcome fear within our communities. We believe we receive when we pray in Jesus Name, Amen!

SCRIPTURE REFERENCES

For God has not given us a spirit of fear, but of power and of love and of a sound mind.

2 Timothy 1:7

The heaven, even the heavens are the Lord's, but the earth He has given to the children of men.

Psalm 115:16

"Be strong and of good courage, do not fear nor be afraid of them; for the Lord your God, He is the one who goes with you. He will not leave you nor forsake you."

Deuteronomy 31:6

"And I will give you the keys of the kingdom of heaven, and whatever you bind on earth will be bound in heaven, and whatever you loose on earth will be loosed in heaven."

Matthew 16:19

A thousand may fall at your side, and ten thousand at your right hand; but it shall not come near you.

Psalm 91:7

The Power of Hearing from God for Our Communities

Father in the name of Jesus we thank You that we have ears to hear what You have to say regarding our communities. We decree that as we walk in Your word on a daily basis, fresh revelation knowledge flows freely through us, unhindered and unchecked by any opposing forces.

We are Your sheep and we hear Your voice, therefore we are not moved by the voice of Satan. We know that the Words we hear produce light and life and we choose to share those same words within our communities.

We decree that we communicate with You Father effectively. We put You in remembrance of Your word, knowing that it shall not return unto You void, but it will accomplish the thing for which it was sent.

So we boldly confess that our ears shall hear a word behind us saying this is the way, walk in it, whenever we turn to the right hand or to the left; confidently knowing that You are always speaking to us, leading, guiding and directing us into all truth.

Father we set ourselves to hear from You and study Your word to get more and more revelation as it relates to our communities. Holy Spirit continually reveals Himself through us and writes Your word on our hearts as we share Your word in our Communities.

We will not move on our own accord, but by Your Spirit. We thank You Father for a prophetic word, a now word concerning the lives of Your people. We decree that Holy Spirit will tell us who to speak to, who to share Your word with, and who to assist at the right time and the right place.

We will not second guess what we hear from You. We will be quick to act on what we hear, knowing that it must come to pass. We thank You for Your peace which surpasses all understanding.

Daily we will feed ourselves with Your word and see the salvation of the Lord in the land of the living. We are spiritual giants in this land and there isn't anything Satan can do about it!

We decree that we hear from You Father regarding our communities because we believe we receive when we pray in Jesus Name, Amen!

Scripture References

"My sheep hear My voice, and I know them, and they follow Me."

John 10:27

Your ears shall hear a word behind you, saying "this is the way, walk in it." Whenever you turn to the right hand or whenever you turn to the left.

Isaiah 30:21

Where there is no counsel, the people fall; but in the multitude of counselors there is safety.

Proverbs 11:14

But be doers of the word, and not hearers only, deceiving yourselves.

James 1:22

The Power of Justice within Our Communities

Father we thank You that we serve a powerful and mighty God who is just! We pray a prayer of justice over our communities. We thank You for being a compassionate and merciful God. We know that You hate injustice. With You there is no compromise or reconciliation with evil. We choose to reside in Your kingdom where justice rule and agree with Your mission to bring love and justice to all because You love justice.

We decree we have communities of righteousness, and fairness. We decree our communities have Your spirit in our hearts that we establish communities of trust, fellowship, justice and peace. Father we ask that You shed light on all darkness in our minds that we may see Your light and think Your thoughts towards one another.

We thank You Father for guiding our communities out of conflict and friction, and bringing us to a place of peace and harmony. That we become bold enough to walk in humility, understanding, purity and sincerity with one another.

Father we know that prayer is our spiritual weapon and we pray for conversion of those who hate justice and every good work. And we ask You to judge those who refuse to be converted.

We bind every temper that makes for violence, ignorance, arrogance and self-assertion within our communities and decree it powerless in the Name of Jesus.

Father heal the differences which divide us, and bring us back into that unity of agape love. Increase the spirit of neighborliness among us all, that in times of danger we may uphold one another, in times of suffering tend one another, and in times of loneliness befriend one another. We choose what is right and stand against that which is evil in our communities. We choose to see others as You see them.

We decree Your kingdom come, Your will be done, on earth as it is in heaven. We decree that there is justice in our communities because we believe we receive when we pray, in Jesus name, Amen.

SCRIPTURE REFERENCES

For I the Lord, love justice; I hate robbery for burnt offering; I will direct their work in truth, and I will make with them an everlasting covenant.

Isaiah 61:8

Thus says the Lord of hosts: 'Execute true justice, show mercy and compassion everyone to his brother.'

Zechariah 7:9

Therefore the Lord will wait, that He may be gracious to you; and therefore He will be exalted, that He may have mercy on you. For the Lord is a God of justice; blessed are all those who wait for Him.

Isaiah 30:18

But the righteous are bold as a lion.

Proverbs 28:1b

The Power of Unity within Our Communities

Father we thank You for the agape love You give us and we choose to share that same love within our communities. When we come together as one, on one accord, we know that You are in the midst. We are a unified community. We stand together in oneness thanking You for restoration in our communities.

We believe we have the power to change the world. We lift up, encourage, and share with our brothers and sisters the knowledge of You so that we are strengthened the more. We take back everything that belongs to us in our communities, in the Name of Jesus.

We know that the prayer of the righteous avails much and as the righteous, we profit in the transformation and restoration of our communities.

As we unite, we refuse to compromise on Your word. We use the Word of God as our final authority and lift up a standard against any plot, scheme or plan Satan has to thwart our unification.

We boldly take back our peace, safety and love that may have been overshadowed by the cares of this world. We cast all those cares on You Father because we know You care for us. We lean not to our own understanding and acknowledge You in all our ways and You will direct our paths.

We take confidence knowing that as we walk in unity, we have the victory. We do not give Satan a foothold in our communities by being in disagreement. We choke the life out of his kingdom and replace it with the Kingdom of God.

Thank You Father that we unite in prayer, and continually devote ourselves to You. We are obligated to unite and will not allow any opposition to stop us from being doers of Your Word and not just hearers only!

Have Your way, Holy Spirit like never before in our lives individually and as a community. We are one in You and shall see the results of this unity now in our communities because we believe we receive when we pray, in Jesus Name, Amen.

Scripture References

Confess your trespasses to one another, and pray for one another, that you be healed. The effective, fervent prayer of a righteous man avails much.

James 5:16

...casting all your care upon Him, for He cares for you.

1 Peter 5:7

Trust in the Lord with all you heart, and lean not on your own understanding; in all your ways acknowledge Him, and He shall direct your paths.

Proverbs 3:5-6

"I do not pray for these alone, but also for those who will believe in Me through their word; that they all may be one, as You Father, are in Me, and I in You; that they also may be one in Us, that the world may believe that You sent Me.

John 17:20-21

But be doers of the word, and not hearers only, deceiving yourselves.

James 1:22

The Power of Walking in Wisdom within Our Communities

Father You said in Your word that if anyone lacks wisdom to ask of You and You shall freely give it to us. So in the Name of Jesus we ask for wisdom within our communities. We decree that we shall walk in wisdom for every situation and circumstance that comes our way. We thank You that Your wisdom is flowing through us, providing guidance, insight and discernment in every area of our lives.

Father Your wisdom in us gives us foresight and understanding concerning all issues. Your wisdom teaches us how to properly manage our time and prioritize our activities; making us effective and efficient in all we do.

Our communities flourish because of Your wisdom. There's peace in our neighborhoods because of Your wisdom. There is vision amongst Your people because they walk in wisdom. We decree that families are restored because of the wisdom of God flowing freely in our communities. We decree that lives are saved because of Your wisdom. As we walk in this wisdom, change is inevitable.

We decree that as we walk in wisdom, we share the joy and love of You toward all people. We are able to make meaningful and significant contributions to others because of this wisdom. Wisdom keeps us from deceived or fooled by others, as it protects us from deceivers and liars and the snares of the enemy. We decree that the steps of the people in our communities are ordered and directed by You Father.

Your word says that Wisdom is the principle thing and in all our getting, get understanding. We decree the same wisdom and exceedingly great understanding You gave Solomon is upon our communities.

We decree that Your wisdom in us keeps us from making poor choices. We are excellent decision-makers because we operate with prudence and discretion. When faced with many possible choices, we decree that God's wisdom in the lives of our communities give us peace in our hearts that we may recognize what are the right decisions that we need to make on a daily basis. We decree that we have the mind of Christ and operate and conduct our lives with Your wisdom Father for the rest of our lives.

We choose to apply our hearts to wisdom and lean on You for continual guidance and direction. We are wise in casting our cares upon You Father and not trying to handle things on our own. We decree Proverbs 3:5-6 as our mantra as we trust in You with all our heart and lean not unto our own understanding, in all our ways we acknowledge You and You will direct our paths.

Have Your way in the lives of Your people like never before Father. We thank You for hearing our prayer and we decree wisdom saturates our communities in Jesus Name, Amen!

SCRIPTURE REFERENCES

If any of you lacks wisdom, let him ask of God, who gives to all liberally and without reproach, and it will be given to him.

James 1:5

Then you will walk safely in your way, and your foot will not stumble.

Proverbs 3:23

Wisdom is the principle thing, therefore get wisdom.

Proverbs 4:7

Let this mind be in you which was also in Christ Jesus

Philippians 2:5

For the LORD gives wisdom; from His mouth come knowledge and understanding

Proverbs 2:6

The Power of Praise for Our Communities

Father in the Name of Jesus we thank You for giving us the breath to praise You on behalf of our communities. For You alone are worthy to be praised and we know that You inhabit the praises of Your people and our praise silences the enemy leaving him powerless and of none effect.

We know that praise is an act of our will and it flows out of our awe and reverence for You Father. We thank You in advance Father that as we praise You we are creating a harmonious symphony in Your ears. When we praise Father we turn our attention off the problems in our communities and focus on You. We decree that perfect peace is the manifestation of our praise!

We choose to obey You Father by praising You. When we praise You Father on behalf of our communities we are restoring our communities back into fellowship with You. As we draw near to You, You draw near to us.

We declare that our praise is changing the hearts of those in our communities that don't know You and are now receptive to receiving Jesus Christ as their Lord and personal Saviour!

Father as we praise You, we decree that we will see the miraculous take place in our communities. Just like the walls of Jericho came crashing down and the prison doors shook open for Paul and Silas, as we praise You on behalf of our communities, we are breaking down barriers and strongholds that have infiltrated our communities.

We will continue to praise You Father in advance for the manifestation of change in our communities. We believe we receive change in Jesus Name, Amen.

SCRIPTURE REFERENCES

Let everything that has breath praise the Lord.
Proverbs 150:6

For the Lord is great and greatly to be praised; He is also to be feared above all gods.
1 Chronicles 16:25

But thou art holy, O thou that inhabitest the praises of Israel.
Psalms 22:3 (KJV)

Out of the mouth of babes and nursing infants You have ordained strength, Because of Your enemies, That You may silence the enemy and the avenger.
Psalms 8:2

Draw near to God and He will draw near to you.
James 4:8

But you are a chosen generation, a royal priesthood, a holy nation, His own special people, that you may proclaim the praises of Him who called you out of darkness into His marvelous light
1 Peter 2:9

The Power of Sharing Jesus within Our Communities

Father in Jesus Name we pray that believers are confident in sharing Jesus within our communities.

We choose to obey the command of Christ and conduct ourselves in a manner worthy of the gospel of Christ.

We decree that we live the abundant life that Jesus died for us to have. Our limitless lifestyle, the words we speak and the good deeds we do, are the Gentile bait that will hook unbelievers to You!

I thank you Father that we are confident and bold in sharing the basics of faith which is the peace of God in our lives that surpasses all understanding, the resurrection of our Lord and Saviour Jesus Christ, the forgiveness of our sins and our personal testimonies of Your goodness towards us. We decree that Romans 8:9-10 will resound loudly throughout our communities changing the posture and position of those that never knew You!

So let us be led by You from this day forward as we share the greatest gift of the Gospel. We choose to be a good example in our communities and faithful witnesses of the faith that lies within us. We decree that we are zealous for Christ in the way that God has gifted us and are always ready to give an answer with eagerness and excitement!

We are making memories as we share the Love of God and His Word. We are making memories as we share our testimonies of the Goodness of God and how He has delivered and transformed our lives with His Word that in turn benefits our communities in knowing that if He did it for us, then He can do it for them too!

We decree that all people will receive Jesus within our communities without hesitation as we use every opportunity to make a mark in our communities that cannot be erased. We believe we receive when we pray in Jesus Name, Amen.

SCRIPTURE REFERENCES

And He said to them, "Go into all the world and preach the gospel to all creation."

Mark 16:15

The thief comes only in order to steal and kill and destroy. I came that they may have and enjoy life, and have it in abundance (to the full, till it overflows).

John 10:10 (AMP)

The wicked flee when no one pursues, but the righteous are bold as a lion.

Proverbs 28:1

If you confess with your mouth the Lord Jesus and believe in your heart that God raised Him from the dead, you will be saved. For with the heart one believes unto righteousness, and with the mouth confession is made unto salvation.

Romans 10:9-10

Preach the word! Be ready in season *and* out of season. Convince, rebuke, exhort, with all longsuffering and teaching.

2 Timothy 4:2

The Power of Healing Sickness and Disease within Our Communities

Heavenly Father we thank You for Your word as it is life to those that find them and health to all their flesh. We choose not to forget all Your mighty benefits and thank You for healing all sickness and disease in our communities. We stand on Your word knowing that nothing is impossible to us and that includes our healing. We know that Jesus has already taken sickness and disease out of our communities when He was beaten and bruised for us. He was our substitute and became sick so we wouldn't have to.

We decree according to Your word that our communities are healed. We receive Your healing power over sickness and disease in our communities.

We speak to every organ in our community's bodies and command all of them to operate and function at 100 percent efficiency, the way You made them. We bind AIDS, Alzheimer's disease, Anemia, Anorexia, Arthritis, Asthma, Bacterial Meningitis, Breast Cancer, Bronchitis, Cancer, Cerebral Palsy, Chronic Fatigue syndrome, the Common Cold, Diabetes, Emphysema, Epilepsy, Food-Borne Illnesses, Gonorrhea, Heart Disease, All types of Hepatitis, HIV, Infertility, Influenza, Iron-Deficiency Anemia, Jaundice, Keloids, Laryngitis, Leukemia, Lung Cancer, Lupus, Lymphoma, Meningitis, Migraines, Mononucleosis, Multiple

Sclerosis, Obesity, Osteoarthritis, Osteoporosis, Parkinson's Disease, Pelvic Inflammatory Disease, Periodontal Disease, Psoriasis, Rheumatism, Rheumatoid Arthritis, Shingles, Sickle-Cell Anemia, Strep Throat, Syphilis, Swine Influenza, Tonsillitis, Tooth Decay, Tumors, Ulcers, Varicose Veins and all other sicknesses and diseases that Satan tried to put on Your people. We come against them and all symptoms in the name of Jesus. We decree they must bow to the name of Jesus. Sickness and disease we call you eradicated from our communities.

We decree that every system in our bodies operate like well-oiled machines. Our nervous system, electrical system, digestive system, circulatory system, lymphatic system, and every other system operate in total and complete harmony with each other. They are free from sickness, disease, growths, and tumors of any kind.

We speak life to and health to our communities. We proclaim that every gland is healthy and whole. Our adrenal gland, thyroid gland, pituitary gland, and all other glands in our bodies operate and function at 100 percent efficiency.

We call on Jehovah Rapha the Lord our Healer. We refuse to be shaken over evil reports of sickness and disease in our communities because we choose to believe the report of the Lord. God's word says that we are healed! We decree that the minds of our communities are renewed to Your word and that they think on things that are true, noble, just, pure, lovely, and of good report. They keep their minds stayed on You Father and You alone. You said that You will keep them in perfect peace. We speak peace now to our communities concerning sickness and disease and thank You in advance for the blood of Jesus covering our bodies and removing all manner of sickness of disease.

We bind Satan and remind him that he is already defeated and he has no authority to put sickness or disease on God's people. Satan is under our feet. We resist him and he must flee. We take full authority of Satan and break the power of any curses or spells that have been spoken over our community's lives. We cast down and break the power of any strategies, maneuvers, or evil plots that the enemy has set in motion to bring destruction to our communities. They shall all come to naught because no weapon formed against us shall ever prosper.

Our communities are strong! We cast our care regarding sickness and disease on You Father and choose not to ever worry or be anxious about anything.

We decree our communities are healed of sickness and disease because we believe we receive when we pray in Jesus Name, Amen!

SCRIPTURE REFERENCES

Bless the Lord, O my soul, and forget not all His benefits: Who forgives all your iniquities, Who heals all your diseases

Psalm 103:2-3

But He *was* wounded for our transgressions, He was bruised for our iniquities; the chastisement for our peace was upon Him, and by His stripes we are healed.

Isaiah 53:5

Because you have made the Lord, who is my refuge, even the Most High, your dwelling place, no evil shall befall you, nor shall any plague come near your dwelling.

Psalm 91:9-10

He sent His word, and healed them, and delivered them from their destructions.

Psalm 107:20

22 So Jesus answered and said to them, "Have faith
in God. **23** For assuredly, I say to you, whoever says
to this mountain, 'Be removed and be cast into the
sea,' and does not doubt in his heart, but believes
that those things he says will be done, he will have
whatever he says. **24** Therefore I say to you,
whatever things you ask when you pray, believe
that you receive *them,* and you will have *them.*

Mark 11:22-24

The Power of Healthy Communities

Father thank You for healthy communities. We decree that our communities are blessed beyond measure and are victorious in every situation or circumstance they come against in Jesus Name!

We declare that our healthy communities stem from healthy relationships within our communities along with renewed minds concerning our communities.

We decree that all are keeping watch over what we allow to enter our hearts and minds. We are mindful of what we read, watch on television and the Internet, as well as what we listen to on the radio and in our conversations with others. We continuously protect our minds by casting down anything that opposes the Word of God.

We refuse to let worry or fear pollute our minds thereby holding us hostage and unable to cope when hit with pressured times. We pressure our pressure by keeping our minds stayed on You Father, speaking Your word and acting on what we believe. We refuse to fill our minds with the poison of gossip, backbiting and jealousy as they are thieves that come to destroy our ability to remain healthy communities.

We decree that our healthy communities are free from break-ins, robberies, assaults, murders, manslaughter, domestic violence, rape, loitering, littering, foreclosures, lack, insufficiency and the like.

We decree blessed communities filled with peace, joy, happiness, prosperity, great educational institutions, and homes where angels can reside and not feel out of place.

Thank You Father for our healthy communities because we believe we receive when we pray in Jesus Name, Amen!

SCRIPTURE REFERENCES

Yet in all these things we are more than conquerors through Him who loved us.

Romans 8:37

I say then: Walk in the Spirit, and you shall not fulfill the lust of the flesh.

Galatians 5:16

You shall also decide *and* decree a thing, and it shall be established for you; and the light [of God's favor] shall shine upon your ways.

Job 22:28

Faith Confession Over Our Communities

Dear Heavenly Father, we come boldly to your throne today confessing Your Word over our communities. As we speak Your Word, we are confident that it will not return void, but it will accomplish everything we speak in our communities! We thank You that Your people are filled with the spirit of wisdom and revelation in the knowledge of You, that the eyes of their understanding is enlightened and they live and conduct themselves in a manner fully pleasing to You.

Father we bind the hand of the enemy in our communities. We bind home invasions, rape, suicide, armed robberies, loitering, illegal drug and sexual activity, lack, poverty, debt, unbelief, theft, and any other demonic influences that may have reared their ugly heads. We loose angels to abide in our communities keeping watch over us, our families, friends, businesses, schools and the like. We loose the peace of God which surpasses all understanding to rule and reign in our communities. We declare that we have sweet sleep as we cast all our cares on You, for we know that You care for us and are perfecting those things which concern us.

God we thank You that Holy Spirit has His way in our communities. We yield ourselves to Holy Spirit and thank Him in advance for His direction and guidance. We thank You that the people are clothed with compassion, kindness, humility, gentleness and patience according to your Word. As we walk in love and unity we decree the peace of Christ rule in our hearts. We decree that our words towards one another build and edify and do not tear down and demeanor.

We thank You for the salvation of souls. We decree that laborers go forth, along with us, to share the Good News to all! We pronounce Your love is shed abroad in the people's hearts.

No weapon formed against our communities shall ever prosper. For our righteousness is of the Lord and whatsoever we do shall prosper. We know that the Kingdom of Heaven suffers violence and the violent takes by force.

So we forcefully take back our communities for the Kingdom of God. Your Word says that one can chase a thousand to flight and two can chase 10,000 to flight, so how much more can we do as Intercessors for Our Communities.

The same power that raised Jesus from the dead resides on the inside of us and NOTHING by any means can hurt or harm us or our communities! Our feet are not made to stumble, and since we walk uprightly we receive all the good things Your word promises us. We decree home values are up, employment is up, and schools are flourishing with talented students, well capable of ascertaining employment and/or starting their own businesses.

We plead the blood of Jesus over our communities. Decreeing and declaring that they are blessed and every single need we have in our communities are met in Jesus Name, Amen!

SCRIPTURES TO READ ALOUD OVER OUR COMMUNITIES

If My people who are called by My name will humble themselves, and pray and seek My face, and turn from their wicked ways, then I will hear from heaven, and will forgive their sin and heal their land.

2 Chronicles 7:14

And my God shall supply all your need according to His riches in glory by Christ Jesus.

Philippians 4:19

Now to Him who is able to do exceedingly abundantly above all that we ask or think, according to the power that works in us.

Ephesians 3:20

"And from the days of John the Baptist until now the kingdom of heaven suffers violence, and the violent take it by force."

Matthew 11:12

No weapon formed against you shall prosper, and every tongue which rises against you in judgment you shall condemn.

Isaiah 54:17

For the Lord God is a sun and shield; the Lord will give grace and glory; no good thing will He withhold from those who walk uprightly.

Psalm 84:11

Prayer of Salvation

As we pray together for our communities, we need to be able to share the prayer of Salvation with those that don't have a personal relationship with Jesus Christ.

Pray this prayer out loud:

Heavenly Father, I know that I am a sinner and I need Jesus Christ in my life. I believe in my heart that Jesus died on the cross just for me and I confess with my mouth that God raised Him from the dead. I repent of my sins and ask that You forgive me and cleanse me from all unrighteousness. I welcome You into my life Jesus. Show me the way. I thank You for saving me and becoming my Lord and personal Savior. In Jesus' name I pray, Amen.

Scripture Reference

If you confess with your mouth the Lord Jesus and believe in your heart that God raised Him from the dead, you will be saved. For with the heart one believes unto righteousness, and with the mouth confession is made unto salvation.

Romans 10:9-10

About the Author

Lillian Joel is a woman of faith, power, love and authority. A person who has welcomed her God ordained assignment to pray for and rebuild our communities with the Word of God. She is an inspirational speaker who is impacting the nation one community at a time.

The audacious teaching she receives as a partner of Spirit of Faith Christian Center in Temple Hills, Maryland under the leadership of Drs. Michael & Deloris Freeman, has taught Lillian to step out of her fear by meditating on God's word and allowing it to be final authority in her life! Her *new* acronym for F.E.A.R. is Fully Excited About Results!

She currently resides in Clinton, Maryland and has one daughter, Brittney.

Made in the USA
Middletown, DE
03 May 2019